A start me up Book

The Seven Wonders
of the Ancient World

By Hans Reichardt

Illustrated by Anne-Lies Ihme, Gerd Werner, Peter Klaucke and Frank Kliemt

*The Temple of Artemis at Ephesus was one of the Seven Wonders of the World.
Only the foundations of this monumental building have survived.*

Tessloff Publishing

Preface

It seems to be part of our nature that we are always looking for extraordinary achievements. The Ancient Greeks used the motto "higher, faster, stronger" to describe the spirit of the Olympic Games, and we seem to feel the same about sporting events today. The search for great achievements isn't limited to sports, however. We want to know who is the richest or most beautiful. We want to know which building is the highest and which car the fastest. We are even interested in apparently pointless records like the biggest submarine sandwich or the longest time spent at the top of a flagpole.

The Seven Wonders of the World were famous for more than breaking a record, however. It is true that the pyramids of Egypt are still — with the exception of the Great Wall of China — the most massive structure ever built by mankind. In its time the Temple of Zeus at Olympia was the biggest religious monument on the Greek mainland. But the statue of Zeus inside the temple didn't break any measurable records. It was famous because of its artistic excellence. Likewise, the Hanging Gardens earned their place on the list of wonders not by their size, but by their outstanding beauty.

The Seven Wonders of the World were admired not simply because they outdid other technological accomplishments of their time, but because of their artistic perfection as well.

This volume of **start me up!** ™ tells the story of the Seven Wonders of the World. Using both pictures and words, it tells how they were built and what they meant to the world back then. It also tells what happened to these wonders and why. Finally, it shows how the Wonders of the World were reflections of their times, and of the people who lived with them.

Volume 3

PUBLISHERS: Tessloff Publishing, Quadrillion Media LLC

EDITOR: Alan Swensen

PICTURE SOURCES:

PHOTOS: R. Ammon, Aichwald: p. 33; Archiv für Kunst und Geschichte, Berlin: pp. 4, 8, 14, 20, 21, 23, 25, 29, 31, 24, 34, 35, 36, 38, 40, 42, 47; Prof. Bauer, Weilheim: pp. 37, 42; J. Blendinger, Nürnberg: p. 29; Bildarchiv preußischer Kulturbesitz, Berlin: pp. 6, 24, 26, 27, 46, 47; dpa, Frankfurt: pp. 6, 7, 8, 9, 14, 22, 28, 44; Prof. Dr. Franke, München: p. 27; Hirmer Fotoarchiv, Munich: p. 18; Fr. Krischen, Weltwunder der Baukunst in Babylon und Jonien: p. 32; Lotos Film, Kaufbeuren: pp. 13, 22, 31, 33, 36, 37; National Museum, Athens: p. 27; Publisher's Archives: pp. 13, 17, 24, 34, 44; Ullstein Bilderdienst, Berlin: pp. 17, 34; ZEFA Bildagentur, Dusseldorf: p. 39;

ILLUSTRATIONS: Anne-Lies Ihme, Peter Klaucke, Frank Kliemt, Gerd Werner

Translated by Sarah Mulholland

COPYRIGHT: © MCMXCVIII Tessloff Publishing, Burgschmietstrasse 2-4, 90419 Nuremberg, Germany
© MCMXCVIII Quadrillion Media LLC, 10105 East Via Linda Road, Suite 103-390, Scottsdale AZ 85258, USA

Visit us on the World Wide Web at http://www.quadrillionusa.com

Library of Congress Cataloging-in-Publication Data is available.

ISBN 1-58185-002-6

Printed in Belgium

Printing 10 9 8 7 6 5 4 3 2 1

Contents

Seven — a Sacred Number

Why is the number seven so special?

Seven was regarded as a special number by many cultures in ancient times. In Egypt and Babylon philosophers and astronomers believed that seven had a special meaning because it was the sum of the "numbers of life" — three and four. Three represented the basis of all life, being the number of figures making up the family unit — father, mother and child. The rain that sustained life came from the winds blowing from the four directions of the compass. The Greeks — and later the Christians — frequently associated the number three with the gods and the number four with the Earth. The ancients believed that all earthly things were made out of four elements — earth, water, air, and fire.

Jews in ancient times also attributed a special importance to seven. In the book of Genesis in the Hebrew scriptures, we read that God created the world in six days, and that he rested on the seventh. In the Ten Commandments, Moses decreed that the seventh day of the week should be a day of rest and should be kept holy. And from this time onwards, Jews believed that seven was a divine number.

In the Jewish religion, the seven arms of this candelabra, the Menora, symbolize the six weekdays and the Sabbath.

4

In fact, since ancient times, there have been countless examples of people finding special meaning in the number seven. Every year the Greeks presented awards honoring their seven best tragic and comic actors. They also revered the "Seven Sages" — seven wise Greeks from the 6th century BC — and so did the Romans. The city of Rome was built on seven hills. In Roman Catholic teachings, there are seven deadly sins: pride, envy, lust, avarice, sloth, gluttony, and wrath. There are also seven holy sacraments: baptism, communion, confession, confirmation, marriage, ordination, and the last rites. In Islam, the final place of enlightenment is known as Seventh Heaven — it is the highest of seven heavens. Then there is the constellation of the Pleiades. The Greeks named it after the seven daughters of Atlas and Pleione. Even though it contains several hundred stars, only six or seven are easily seen without the aid of a telescope.

The mysterious number seven shows up everywhere in fairy tales as well. The knight Bluebeard, for example, had seven wives. Snow White lived with the Seven Dwarves, and they of course lived behind the Seven Mountains. There was also the courageous tailor who managed to kill "seven with one blow," though it was only seven flies! We could find countless other examples.

The Seven Wonders of the World — some of the greatest and most famous works of art and architecture in the

Who first described the Seven Wonders of the World?

ancient Mediterranean world — are one of the oldest examples of the number seven being used in a special way. A Phoenician author, Antipatros of Sidon, wrote the first known account of the Seven Wonders of the World. He lived during the 2nd century BC. His book wasn't a scholarly study of the wonders, however, or even an art book. It was a travel guide, something like a "Fodor Guide" to the ancient world.

On his journeys — if he actually took such journeys and wasn't just reporting what others told him — Antipatros basically followed the established trade routes of the known world at that time. He found only one of these world wonders in mainland Greece — the statue of Zeus at Olympia. Two of the wonders he described were from Asia Minor: the Temple of Artemis at Ephesus, and the tomb of King Mausolus of Halicarnassus. The Colossus, a statue of the sun

- Olympia
- Ephesus
- Halicarnassus
- Rhodes
- Babylon
- Alexandria
- Cairo
- Giza

god Helios, was on the island of Rhodes. Two more wonders came from the continent of Africa: the Pharos at Alexandria and the Khufu Pyramid at Giza. The final wonder was from the Near East: the Hanging Gardens of Queen Semiramis in the ancient city of Babylon.

Antipatros doesn't even mention some of the famous buildings that were actually much closer to home — almost at his doorstep, so to speak — for example, the Acropolis in Athens. After all, his book was supposed to be a travel guide for educated Greeks — and he certainly didn't have to call their attention to the Acropolis!

Before archaeologists excavated the remains of Babylon, people formed fantastic images of the Tower of Babel. One of the most famous of these images is this painting by Pieter Bruegel the Elder.

The Acropolis — seen here overlooking present-day Athens.

<table>
<tr><td>

Why isn't the Tower of Babel one of the Seven Wonders?

</td></tr>
</table>

In his list, Antipatros included only "wonders" that could still be visited. The Tower of Babel was certainly one of the great architectural works of its day, but it was already a ruin in Antipatros' time and not of interest to "tourists." The beauty-loving Greeks didn't think ruins were worthy of admiration.

Enthusiasm for the Seven Wonders didn't last very long. With the rise of Christianity, interest in antiquity faded. Except for the pyramids, the Seven Wonders were now ruins and soon fell into oblivion.

If it weren't for the Arabs the Seven Wonders of the World might have been entirely forgotten by now. It was Arab scholars who collected the writings of ancient Greek authors and preserved them for later generations.

Finally, with the beginning of the Renaissance, Europe again became interested in the ancient world. Then, in the 17th century, the Austrian architect Johann Fischer von Erlach (1606–1723) reintroduced Europe to the Seven Wonders of the World. Using the writings of ancient authors, he published descriptions of the Seven Wonders of the World. It was another 200 years, however, before scientists began digging up artifacts from classical antiquity. When these artifacts went on display, modern people were able to see more clearly what the ancient inhabitants of the Mediterranean world had accomplished. At last, the Seven Wonders of the World had been rediscovered.

THE ACROPOLIS was already the site of a fortress more than 3,000 years ago. It provided protection for its inhabitants and was also the residence of the king of Athens. After the Persians had destroyed Athens in 480 BC, the Athenians immediately started rebuilding their city. In a period of 40 years the great temples of the Acropolis were rebuilt: the Parthenon, the Propylaea, the Erechtheum, and the temple honoring the goddess of victory, Athena Nike. Even though these buildings have long been ruins, they have served as models for monumental public buildings even in our times.

The Pyramid of Khufu

Which is the first of the Seven Wonders of the World?

The Pyramid of Khufu at Giza in Egypt is the oldest of the Seven Wonders of the World. It is also the only one that has survived more or less intact up to the present. Because of its size it is also called the Great Pyramid and is listed first among the Seven Wonders. It was named after its builder, Pharaoh Khufu (approx. 2551–2528 BC) – his name in Greek was Cheops. Except for the Great Wall of China, the Pyramid of Khufu is the largest structure ever built by man. It is 480 feet high – the same height as a fifty-story skyscraper. Its base covers an area of 251 yards square – an area so big that the five largest churches in the world could fit on it at the same time: St. Peter's in Rome, St. Paul's and Westminster Abbey in London, and the Cathedrals of Florence and Milan. The amount of stone used to build the Pyramid of Khufu is equal to the amount of stone used in all the churches built in Germany in the past thousand years!

Immediately after the death of his father, Snefru, the young Pharaoh Khufu – "Pharaoh" was the title of the ancient Egyptian kings – began building the pyramid. Like all of his predecessors since King Zoser (about 2605–2530 BC), he wanted to be buried in a pyramid. Like all of his predecessors, he also wanted his pyramid to be bigger, more beautiful, and more splendid than all the previous ones.

Complex preparations had to be made before the first of more than two million limestone blocks could be brought to the west bank of the Nile. First of all, a suitable site had to be found. The pyramid weighs about 6,300,000 tons. They had to find a site where the ground was very solid, or the pyramid

Originally all three pyramids at Giza — the Khufu, the Khafre and the Menkaure Pyramid (seen here right to left) — were described as World Wonders. Today, however, only the Khufu or Great Pyramid is generally recognized as one of the seven greatest engineering feats of ancient times.

The step-pyramid at Saqqara, near Memphis (southwest of Cairo), was built in 2600 BC as the tomb of Pharaoh Zoser. Construction lasted 29 years.

would have sunk into the ground under its own weight. They found such a site south of the modern-day Egyptian capital, Cairo. The place they chose was part of a desert plateau four miles west of the village of Giza. It provided a solid, rock foundation that could support the weight of the pyramid.

How was the Pyramid of Khufu built?

First they leveled the foundation. To do this they built a watertight wall of sand and stones around the proposed base. Then they cut a grid of small canals into this rock base, making it look like a gigantic chessboard. They filled these canals with water, marked the water level on the sides of the canals, and then drained the canals. Stonemasons then cut away any rock above the line of the water level. The canals were then filled in, and the foundation of the pyramid was finished.

About 4,000 people — artists, architects, stonemasons, and other craftsmen — worked for approximately ten years just to complete these preparations. Now they could start with the actual construction of the pyramid.

According to the Greek historian Herodotus (490–425 BC), the construction took another twenty or so years. He reports that around 100,000 people worked on the massive tomb. His account also indicates that 1,600 talents (about $12 million in today's currency) were spent just for garlic, radishes, and onions — important ingredients for the workers' meals.

Many researchers today doubt that Herodotus' count of the

The ivory statue of Pharaoh Khufu is the only surviving image of the king. He is wearing the crown of Lower Egypt and holding a ceremonial branch.

During the construction of the seven-tiered Maydum Pyramid near Memphis the outer layer of Tura limestone slid down because the sides were too steep. The sliding stones probably caused the death of many workers. The monument was never finished.

THE NILE was the life-source of the great Egyptian civilization. This mighty river is 4,132 miles long from its source in Burundi to its mouth at the Mediterranean Sea — the fertile Nile Delta. Without the Nile's water Egypt would have been as infertile as the Sahara Desert. Every year the

Nile floods for many weeks and deposits mineral-rich silt on the bordering farmlands. It is also — and always has been — an important waterway. Even stone blocks weighing tons could be relatively easily transported by boat or raft. For this reason the Greek historian Herodotus (484–425 BC) called Egypt "a gift of the Nile."

workers is accurate. According to them there wouldn't have been enough room for so many people at the building site. On an organized project like this, if there had been any more than 8,000 workers, they would have started to get in each other's way.

Egypt was a wealthy country at the time the pyramid was built. Every year, from the end of June to the beginning of November, the Nile River flooded its banks and covered the fields along the river with a thick layer of silt. This silt transformed the desert sands into fertile farmland. In a good year, they might have as many as three harvests. From June to November, however, the farmers couldn't work their land. They were therefore happy when a royal scribe appeared in the village each July to record the names of any who wanted to work on the pyramid.

Almost everyone wanted to —

Who worked on the construction of the pyramid?

the work was not forced labor but rather voluntary service. There were two reasons for this. First, every man who participated received lodging, clothing, food, and a small wage for as long as he was working there. Four months later, when the River Nile receded again and the fields became workable, the farmers could return to their villages. In addition to this, however, every Egyptian considered it an honor and duty to help build the pharaoh's tomb. All who assisted in the great project believed they were sharing in some small degree in the immortality of the god-king. Each year at the end of June then, masses of farmers would stream towards Giza. There they were

quartered in temporary barrack-like lodgings and assigned to squads of eight men each. Now the work could begin.

The men crossed the Nile in ferries and marched to the stone quarry. Here they broke a block of stone from the rock face. Then, using hammers, chisels, saws and drills they cut the block until its height and length were between 2.6 and 4.75 feet, depending on the instructions they were given. Using ropes and levers, each squad then heaved "its" block onto a wooden sled. They then dragged the sled to the banks of the Nile, pulling it over a track made from

Every summer the Nile flooded its banks, covering the fields with fertile river mud. Since the fields were unworkable during this period, Egyptian farmers went to Giza and worked on the pyramids.

not yet been invented. Using ropes and levers, the workers pushed and pulled the sled and block up a wide spiral ramp built with bricks made of Nile mud. At the top of the previously completed part of the pyramid, they pushed the block into the precise position indicated by the master builder.

The taller the pyramid grew, the longer and steeper the ramp became. In addition, the workspace at the top of the pyramid also became smaller. The work therefore became more and more difficult.

Then came the most dangerous part of the job. The workers pulled the pyramidon — the 30-foot-high capstone — up the ramp and set it in place. This part of the work alone probably cost many workers their lives.

What was the most dangerous part of the work?

After twenty years of work, the core of the pyramid was completed. It consisted of 128 layers, and was almost 200 feet taller than the

logs. A small sailboat was used to transport the men and the stone block — which might weigh as much as 7.5 tons — to the opposite bank of the Nile.

On the other side, the men hauled the stone block to the building site, once again along a track paved with logs. The next part of the work was the most difficult, since cranes and "block and tackle" had

Cross-section of the Pyramid of Khufu
a= entrance, as in all pyramids, on the north side; b= large corridor; c= unfinished chamber; d= rising corridor; e= Great Hall;
f= corridor to the Middle Chamber;
g= Queen's Chamber; h= connecting shaft created by grave robbers; i= corridor with small antechambers; k= King's Chamber; l= hollow spaces to reduce the structural load above the King's Chamber.

airshaft
airshaft
l
i
k
g
e
f
h
d
a
b
original polished limestone panels
shaft
c

United States Capitol. At this stage, the pyramid looked much as it does today — a mountain of steps. The pyramid was not yet finished, however. The steps were filled in with stones so that the pyramid was no longer "stepped," though it still had a rough surface.

As the last step, the workers covered the four triangular outer surfaces with gleaming white limestone slabs. The edges of the slabs were so precisely cut that you couldn't even fit a knife blade in the crack between two stones once they were in place. Even from just a few feet away the pyramid looked like a gigantic mountain made from a single piece of stone. Using the hardest grindstones, workers polished these outer slabs until they shone like mirrors. Eyewitnesses reported that Khufu's monument gleamed mysteriously — in both sunlight and moonlight — like an enormous crystal, lit from within.

The Khufu pyramid is not solid stone throughout, however. In the core of the structure there is a network of passageways. These passages lead via a 154-foot-long passage — the "Great Gallery" — to the King's Chamber. The King's Chamber is 35 feet long, 17 feet wide and 18 feet high. The walls of the chamber are covered with a granite facing but are without any decoration. There is a large, granite sarcophagus in the chamber, but it is empty and the lid is missing. The sarcophagus must have been carried into the room while the pyramid was still being built, since it couldn't fit through any of the passageways. King's chambers like this have been found in almost all of the Egyptian pyramids. They served as the final resting-place of the pharaoh.

THE ARCHITECT of the first pyramids was Imhotep. He was employed at the court of Pharaoh Zoser (or Djoser) around 2600 BC. Imhotep was one of the first geniuses in the history of the world. He was an important writer and physician, and even 3,000 years later was still revered in Egypt as a god of healing. Tradition says that he was the inventor

of stone buildings (using cut rocks for building instead of clay bricks that had been dried in the sun). The pyramid that Imhotep built for Zoser did not have a smooth exterior. Instead it was stepped — it had six tiers. It required 900,000 tons of stone and reached a height of 197 feet!

When a pharaoh died, the Egyptians took his body across the Nile to the valley temple. Here they embalmed the body. Then they moved it to its final resting-place in the pyramid.

How was a pharaoh buried?

When a pharaoh died, his body was first carefully embalmed and then laid out in the burial chamber of the pyramid. The inner organs, which had already been removed, were preserved in airtight vessels called "Canopic" jars. These were placed next to the sarcophagus in the burial chamber.

While the pharaoh's mortal shell lay in its final resting-place in the pyramid, his "Ka" left the burial chamber. According to Egyptian belief, Ka was the second self, a kind of mirror image of the living person. It left the body at death and could then move freely between this world and the next. The Ka left the burial chamber and climbed the outer surface of the pyramid — so smooth that no mortal could climb it — to the very top. Here the sun god Re, the father of all pharaohs, waited in his sun boat. In this boat the dead king began his journey into immortality.

In recent years many researchers have begun to doubt that the Great Pyramid was actually the final resting-place of Pharaoh Khufu. They offer three reasons for their doubts:

First, the burial chamber is completed undecorated, contrary to the usual practice of the times.

Second, the sarcophagus, which was supposed to hold the corpse of the dead king, is unfinished — it is roughly cut and the lid is missing.

Third, and perhaps most significantly, there are two narrow airshafts leading from the burial chamber through small openings in the pyramid's outer surface to the open air. The dead, however, don't need air — and this, too, is important evidence that the Khufu pyramid was not a burial monument.

The picture above shows the entrance to the Pyramid of Khufu. The one below shows the burial chamber containing the granite sarcophagus. Since the chamber walls are unpainted and have no inscriptions, researchers do not believe that Khufu was buried here.

For more than 3,500 years the interior of the Great Pyramid remained untouched by human hand, protected by the carefully walled-up entrances — and also by the Egyptians' belief that kings' tombs were guarded by spirits that killed all intruders.

Not until much later did grave robbers break into the Khufu Pyramid. The first to enter the Khufu pyramid was Caliph Abd Allah al-Ma'mun (813 to 833 BC), a son of Harun al Raschid. He ordered a tunnel broken open into the burial chamber, hoping to find great treasures like those found in other kings' tombs. But he found nothing — nothing, that is, except an 11-inch-thick layer of bat dung covering the floor and walls. This "discovery" made the Khufu pyramid uninteresting as far as treasure seekers and grave robbers were

Who first broke into the Pyramid of Khufu?

Courtyard of a mosque in the oldest quarter of Cairo. Builders often took white limestone surfacing from the pyramids for such buildings.

concerned. Not for other kinds of robbers, however. In 1168 AD, Arabs set fire to part of Cairo and completely destroyed it to prevent it from falling into the hands of the Christian Crusaders. As they were rebuilding their city, the Egyptians tore off the gleaming white limestone slabs that made up the pyramid's outer surface and used them to build new houses. You can still see these slabs in many of the mosques in the old city. Only the stepped core of the pyramid remained standing — just as it appears today to admiring tourists.

These robbers also took the tip of the pyramid, the pyramidon, and the top layers of the structure. Today, because of this, the height of the pyramid is no longer 474.5 feet, but only 452 feet. The tip of the pyramid is now a square platform with sides approximately 32 feet long.

In the 12th century, Egyptians tore off the gleaming limestone surfaces and used them in building houses.

THE GREAT PYRAMID OF KHUFU may be the largest pyramid but is certainly not the only one in Egypt. Next to it is the Pyramid of Khufu's son, Khafre. It is six feet shorter — 446 feet tall — but because it was built on higher ground it seems taller. The Sphinx, a 66-foot high sculpture with the head of Khafre on the body of a lion is part of the complex. The tomb of Khafre's son, Menkaure — the third of the large pyramids — is only 230 feet high. Dozens of other, much smaller pyramids are scattered around Egypt, though many of them have been rendered almost unrecognizable by weathering.

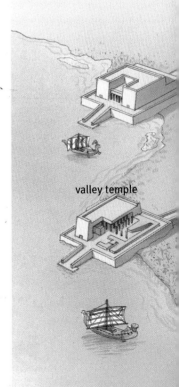
valley temple

For about 1,000 years, between 2630 and 1640 BC, the Egyptian kings built pyramid-shaped structures for their tombs. These pyramids were originally part of more extensive groupings of buildings. Right next to the pyramid there was a funerary temple that was divided into two sections. The outer part contained the entrance and the courtyard, and the inner part was filled with statues and food supplies for the pharaoh in the hereafter. Trenches with luxurious barges were kept there for his transportation into the underworld. Often smaller pyramids for queens were part of the complex of buildings. A very high wall surrounded the whole site. Near it were simple tombs, the "mastabas" of priests and high officials of the pharaoh, who were buried there to serve him in the afterlife. A small paved trail led from the funerary temple to the Nile. On the banks of the Nile there was a second temple and a landing for boats bringing funeral processions from the other side.

All these buildings are gone. Most of them were torn down thousands of years ago and their stones used in other buildings. Only the great pyramids and a few of the smaller ones have survived the 4,000 years that have passed since they were built.

> ## Did the pyramids always stand alone in the desert sands?

The pyramid complex at Giza. In the foreground are the graves ("mastabas") of high officials and priests. The smaller pyramids beyond the mastabas were for the queens. A long covered causeway leads from the valley temple on the Nile to the mortuary temple with its hall of pillars and on to the king's pyramid.

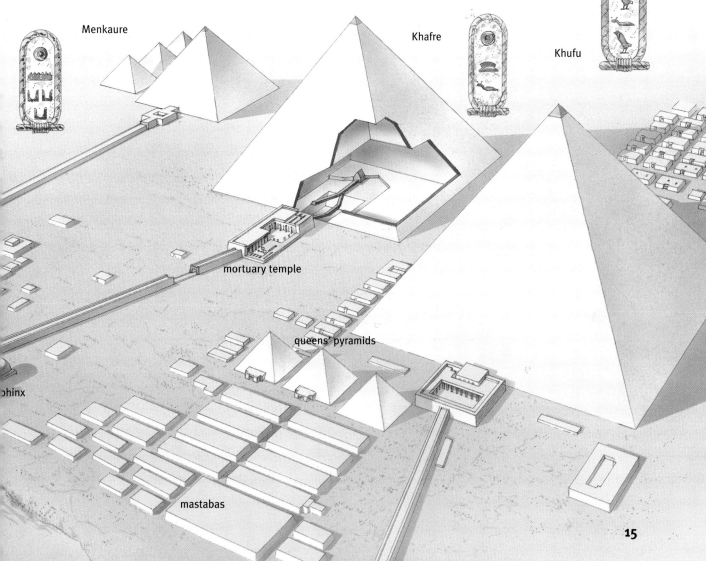

Menkaure

Khafre

Khufu

mortuary temple

queens' pyramids

Sphinx

mastabas

Against the backdrop of the dry Babylonian landscape, the Hanging Gardens seemed like a miracle created by human hands.

The Hanging Gardens of Semiramis

In 1898 the German archaeologist Peter Koldewey began to look for the remains of the ancient city of Babylon. He began his search on the banks of the River Euphrates, about 50 miles south of Baghdad in what is now Iraq. Babylon – the "Babel" of the Hebrew Bible – existed for more than 3,000 years, and three times in the course of its history it was entirely destroyed and then built up again. Finally, during the 6th and 5th centuries BC, under the rule of the Persians and Macedonians, it declined and fell to ruin.

> **Which buildings made Babylon famous?**

Babylon was the first cosmopolitan city in the history of the world. It was famed above all for three outstanding structures. Given the technology available in ancient Babylon, they were truly sensational: the Tower of Babel, the

THE CITY OF BABYLON is also famous because of the Tower of Babel. According to the Biblical story, the people of that time became arrogant and thought they could build a tower that reached all the way to heaven. In order to prevent this, God gave each tribe a different language so they could no longer communicate and work together.

ROBERT KOLDEWEY

(1855–1925) led the excavations at Babylon from 1899 to 1917 for the German Orientalist Society. The German architect and archaeologist had already led successful digs in Mesopotamia. He had to leave the excavations when the British conquered Baghdad during the First World War.

Robert Koldewey (center) and native helpers in the search of the Hanging Gardens of Semiramis

massive walls that encircled the city, and the Hanging Gardens of Semiramis.

Koldewey devoted eighteen years of his life to the project. The work required tremendous resources. In order to cope with the huge mountains of dirt and rubble from the excavation, he had to have an entire railway sent from Europe and set up at the digging site — and in the end, he was successful.

He found the Babylonian Tower, a huge stepped temple with a massive interior — built in honor of the Babylonian state god, Marduk. The tower was originally about 300 feet tall and rested on a base 300 feet by 300 feet. All that was left of the tower now, however, were a few sections of foundation walls and an enormous pile of rubble.

Koldewey also found the wall that had surrounded the city of Babylon. The size of the wall inspired wonder throughout the ancient world: the top was so wide that two horse-drawn wagons could easily drive side-by-side on it! The wall had enclosed not only the city and the palace complex,

Almost nothing remains of the Tower of Babel. Where it once stood palm trees now grow between piles of rubble and mud holes.

but also a large stretch of grazing land. This enclosure was probably intended as a fortified refuge for the rural population in case enemies attacked. Again however, Koldewey found only the foundation walls — some almost 40 feet high — and enormous mounds of rubble. But where were the famous Hanging Gardens?

After many years of searching for the gardens unsuccessfully, one day the German researcher stumbled across a building that was unlike any he had ever seen before. It was located in the northeast corner of the extensive palace complex and buried under

What did Koldewey discover beneath the rubble of the city?

The excavations carried out by Koldewey and other explorers allow us to form a rough idea of what the Babylonian tower may have looked like. It was a solid tiered temple, built on a base 300 feet by 300 feet, and with a height of 300 feet.

many feet of debris. The foundations consisted of twelve narrow chambers, all of them the same size. In contrast to all the other structures discovered in Babylon, these were made of cut stone. The chambers were positioned on either side of a central corridor. The arched ceilings over the chambers were made of fired bricks and were so massive that they must have been intended to bear heavy loads. The walls and pillars were up to 22 feet thick. This unusual type of construction was not the only striking thing he found, however. Right next to these vaulted chambers Koldewey discovered a well underneath the rubble. It was made up of a central circular shaft

Excavations in Babylon. The picture above shows the foundations of the temple of Marduk.

and two smaller rectangular ones. The mechanism for drawing water — it was probably made of wood and thick rope — had not survived.

For a long time, Koldewey puzzled over the purpose of these underground vaults and then found the answer. In several Greek and Roman texts, and also in clay tablets from ancient Babylonian, he found indications that cut stone had only been used in two places in Babylon — in the north wall of the "Qasr" — the king's castle — and in the "Hanging Gardens of Semiramis." Koldewey had already found the cut stone of the Qasr, and therefore these underground vaults had to belong to the famous Hanging Gardens.

From the extensive literature about ancient Babylon, Koldewey was now able to form a picture of what the gardens of Semiramis might have looked like. Above the cellar vaults there had probably been a terraced structure, with each terrace some 16 feet higher than the one below it. Each terrace had a floor made of stone beams 18 feet long and four-and-a-half feet wide. On top of this floor came a layer of reeds mixed with bitumen, and above this a double layer of fired bricks. The cracks between the bricks were sealed with plaster. Next this surface was covered with sheets of lead, which served to protect the

From the solid construction of the underground vaults Koldewey concluded that the gardens were built directly on top of them.

BITUMEN, a kind of tar, was already in use over 6,000 years ago in Mesopotamia. They valued this sticky, black material as a waterproof mortar for building foundations where groundwater might be a problem. The Babylonians probably used it to seal joints in the Hanging Gardens. Bitumen occurs in nature when heat or pressure forces the lighter elements in petroleum to evaporate. The Egyptians used bitumen in the mummification process for the bodies of poorer citizens. They also believed it was a universal cure. Today, large quantities of tar are produced as a by-product when oil is refined. It is often mixed with fill material and used for surfacing roads — we then call it asphalt.

SCIENCE owes many of its fundamental principles to the Babylonians. We know this from clay tablets excavated at Babylon, Ur, Nineveh, and other Mesopotamian cities. The tables contain writing — in the Sumerian language — that was pressed into the clay while it was still wet. Scholars in the highly developed cultures along the Euphrates had already discovered what we now call the Pythagorean theorem. They made calculations using mathematical roots and exponents, and solved equations with multiple unknowns. They developed counting systems in base 12 and 60 that we still use today for measuring angles and time. They had a very accurate calendar and could predict eclipses. They also had considerable knowledge of medicine and chemistry.

foundations against humidity. Finally, on top of the lead, there was a layer of soil 10 feet thick — the actual garden. The soil was deep enough to support even tall trees.

After he returned to Berlin, Koldewey triumphantly announced: "I have found the Hanging Gardens." It wasn't long, however, until some began to question his triumph. Other scholars, also drawing on ancient texts, tried to prove that the Hanging Gardens couldn't possibly have been where Koldewey suggested. Some claimed the gardens had been next to rather than within the fortified city, others believed that they had been neither next to nor within the walls, but in fact some distance away, directly on the banks of the Euphrates River. Some even

Why do some people question Koldewey's discovery?

claimed the gardens weren't on the banks of the river, but actually built over it — on something like a wide bridge spanning the river.

Which of these theories is right and which wrong, no one knows. We will probably never know for sure. It is also unclear why the gardens are attributed to Semiramis. Semiramis was a legendary Babylonian-Assyrian queen who lived several hundred years before the Hanging Gardens were built — if she ever really existed at all. Of course, the queen who lived in Babylon at the time when the gardens were built may have been named Semiramis too — but there is no evidence that this is the case.

The Hanging Gardens — the second wonder on Antipatros' list — are thus the least documented of the Seven Wonders. All we know for sure is that they were in Babylon and that King Nebuchadrezzar (605–562 BC) built them — the king who led Babylon into the most successful period in its history.

When his father Nabopolassar died in 605 BC, Nebuchadrezzar II became king. In the course of many wars he made his kingdom into the leading power in its day. At the same time he transformed his capital city into the largest, most modern, and most splendid city in the ancient world. In the course of only a few decades Babylon became the greatest city of its time. King Nebuchadrezzar, however, spent the majority of his 43-year reign on military cam-

Who transformed Babylon into a leading world power?

soil
lead
bricks
bitumen and reeds
stone beams

An ingenious system of layered materials as a foundation for each terrace and a cleverly designed network of canals linking the terraces kept the plants from drying out.

The double arches of the Ishtar Gate were approximately 130 feet high and formed the entrance to the Processional Way that led to the main temple of the goddess. They were richly decorated with reliefs of glazed tiles.

THE OLD TESTAMENT depicts Nebuchadrezzar as a tyrant because he held the people of Judah captive in Babylon. This may have been propaganda, however. According to other sources the Jews in Babylon fared quite well. They were not treated like prisoners but had their own administration and could practice their professions. Many even achieved great wealth. They occasionally had to do hard labor, but so did the Babylonians themselves. Some records suggest that when the Persians conquered Babylon and permitted the Jews to go home, the majority of them stayed.

paigns. He battled rebellious Assyrians in the north, Syrians in the west, and, above all, the Jews in Palestine, who had allied themselves with Egypt.

Nebuchadrezzar rebuilt Esagila, the chief sanctuary of the Babylonian god Marduk, and created a magnificent complex around the temple. He also restored and completed the 300-foot-high tiered tower of Etemenanki, also a temple of Marduk, which became known in history as "the Tower of Babel." Nebuchadrezzar also had a monumental processional avenue designed as a setting for the extravagant festivals that were held almost daily and that made the city a symbol of decadence. In size and opulence it was without rival in the world at that time. Nebuchadrezzar built two huge royal palaces and erected two rings of fortified walls around the city.

Large gates and wide avenues led through these walls into the city, passing the many newly built palaces and temples. The gate and avenue dedicated to Ishtar, the goddess of battle and of love, were

decorated with images of animals made from glazed bricks. According to an old text, Babylon had 53 temples of the great gods, 55 smaller temples of Marduk, 300 more small temples dedicated to the earth gods, 500 more to the sky gods, 180 altars to Ishtar, and 200 more to various other gods.

Glazed-tile reliefs, like the lion pictured above, lined the Processional Way leading to the temple of Ishtar.

In 587 BC Nebuchadrezzar II destroyed Jerusalem and took the Jews to Babylon, into the "Babylonian Captivity." He probably did so because he needed their labor in the expansion of his capital city. In 539 BC the Persian king Cyrus conquered Babylon and allowed the Jews to return to their homeland.

A recent model of the Tower of Babel.

The Ishtar Gate, part of the massive wall around Babylon, as reconstructed by Koldewey. Ishtar was the Babylonian goddess of love and war.

Visitors from all over the ancient world came to the city to marvel at its size and splendor. In the market places merchants traded fabrics from Phoenicia, incense from Arabia, carpets and precious stones from Persia, tin from Britain, silver from Spain, copper and gold from Egypt, and ivory and spices from India. There were also countless artists and craftsmen who were skilled at working with metals and producing glass and fabrics. There were many doctors who practiced ancient healing arts and even performed difficult operations. Since Babylonians believed whatever happened to humans was the will of the gods, they said prayers and held ceremonial rites before all medical procedures.

Why were the Hanging Gardens built?

It was during this time that the Hanging Gardens of Semiramis were created. They were probably a gift from Nebuchadrezzar to his wife, a Persian princess — whose name may or may not have been Semiramis, the name of the legendary queen. The records report that the king had the gardens built to compensate his wife for his frequent absences. They were probably also meant to relieve her of the monotony of the plains along the Euphrates, and to

This ancient fresco from the wall of a Theban grave shows an Egyptian garden. Date palms surround a pond where fish and ducks swim.

en terraces, each constituting a garden in itself — this is why the plural is used, "Hanging Gardens." Nevertheless, the seven gardens still formed a unified whole. At the outer edge of each terrace there were thousands of vines and trailing plants, which spilled over and down to the next lower terrace, making seven individual gardens into one great garden. It must have looked like a large, green, steeply sloped mountain with countless trees, hedges, bushes, and flowers that looked as if they were hanging or hovering — hence the name "Hanging" Gardens.

The king ordered his armies to bring back specimens of unknown plants they came across during military campaigns in distant lands. Caravans and ships arriving in Babylon often brought new specimens from far lands. Thus a huge, colorful garden developed — the world's first botanical garden.

In the summer, when temperatures could reach 120° F, slaves worked especially hard pumping water to the many canals flowing from the highest terrace down through the gardens. There were streams and waterfalls, and ponds with ducks and frogs. While the relentless summer heat engulfed the rest of the city, the Hanging Gardens blossomed, unaffected by heat or lack of water. It may have been this contrast that earned the gardens the honor of second place on the list of the Seven Wonders of the World.

GARDENS were an extremely important part of the culture of the ancient Near East. No wonder, when one considers the contrast between cool gardens with their fountains and fragrant flowers and the dry, dusty desert. When the Greeks encountered these gardens during the campaigns of Alexander the Great they felt that their own word "gortos," which they used for their domestic vegetable gardens, was unsuitable. They used the word "paradeisos," adapted

from an old Persian expression, for these green oases in the desert. This is the origin of our word "paradise."

remind her of the wooded mountains of her Persian homeland.

Lavish palace gardens in desert locations were nothing new. In Nineveh the Assyrian king Sennacherib (705-681 BC), who was reputedly mad, had ordered holes carved out of the rocky ground around the Temple of the Assyrian god Assur. He linked the holes together by a system of underground canals, in which water flowed, and then filled them with soil, creating the basis for a garden. The Assyrian gardens were no match for the gardens of Semiramis, however.

Babylonian writers — and later Greek and Roman writers as well — agreed: in the beauty of the structure and the variety of plants displayed, the Gardens of Semiramis were without equal in the entire world of that day. There were probably sev-

> **What did the Hanging Gardens look like?**

The Statue of Zeus at Olympia

To which god were the Olympic Games dedicated?

Every fourth summer, a strange thing happened in ancient Greece. The Athenians might be waging war against the Spartans, or the Ionians against the Thebans; two armies might be arrayed opposite each other, ready for battle; perhaps cities were being besieged, captured, and plundered – young Athenians, young Spartans, and other young men from all over Greece passed by the battling armies and besieged cities as if none of it mattered to them. They were on their way to Olympia, a site sacred to Zeus, 156 miles southwest of Athens. For there the great festival was once again about to begin, and as long as it lasted, peace reigned in the area surrounding the sacred grove. Everyone taking part in the festival was guaranteed safe conduct on the way to and from Olympia. Wars in more distant regions, on the other hand, were allowed to continue. Zeus, the highest of the Greek gods, demanded it thus – since the festival was held in his honor. In fact, it was this mighty hurler of lightning who had ordered that the festival be held.

According to legend, Zeus' father, Cronos, lived on a hill above Olympia. An oracle had warned him that one of his sons would rob him of his throne. In response, Cronos devoured all his children as soon as they were born. When his sixth child, Zeus, was born, however, Cronos' wife resorted to cunning. In place of her newborn child, she wrapped a stone in a blanket, and Cronos, in a blind rage, swallowed it. Zeus was kept at a secret place, and there he grew up. When

The statue of Zeus sculpted by Phidias of Athens is considered one of the Seven Wonders. It stood in the cella of the temple of Olympia. The figure was 40 feet high and richly decorated with gold and ivory. The throne was made of ivory.

he was fully-grown, he resolved to take revenge for his father's terrible deeds. First, he gave him something that caused him to vomit. Out of Cronos' mouth came the five sons and daughters born before Zeus, all still alive. This led to a ruthless fight between father and son. Zeus won and cast his father into Tartarus, the hell of ancient times. From then on, Zeus was the sole ruler of Olympus, king of the gods and of humans, and god of the weather. In commemoration of his victory, he established the competition at Olympia.

And so a great festival was celebrated every four years — in 776 BC for the first time — a festival that mixed religious

According to Greek mythology, Zeus owed his life to a cunning trick played by his mother Rhea. Her husband Cronos devoured his children as soon as they were born. When Zeus was born, his mother wrapped a stone in the blanket instead of her newborn baby, and handed it to Cronos. He didn't notice the deception and swallowed the stone. The picture shows a fragment of a vase with an illustration from this story.

> **When did the first Olympic Games take place?**

observances with bitterly fought athletic competitions. The celebrations were called the "Olympic Games," and the span of time between two games was called an "Olympiad." Each Olympiad was given a name — after one of the winners in the most recent competition. In modern terms, it was like calling the four years between the Olympic Games of 1996 and 2000 the "Carl Lewis Olympiad."

The first Olympic Games were held on a small scale. Only the young men from the surrounding area made their way to the sacred grove at the foot of Cronos' hill to test their skills in athletic competition. In the beginning the only buildings there were a treasury, a building where the Olympic flame was kept, a temple for Zeus and his wife, Hera, and a small altar.

Three hundred years later Olympia looked very different. The modest local games had become the most important Panhellenic competition, and each time the best athletes and thousands of spectators streamed in from every part of Greece. Since there were no permanent houses, they slept in tents. Merchants set up their stands and poets read from their works to large and discerning audiences. Where once there had been a small sacred grove there was now a forest of statues, large and small temples, and altars — making Olympia the most sacred place in the cult of Zeus.

The painting on this jug shows an Olympic broad-jumper with jumping weights in his hands. Ancient broad-jumping techniques were very different than modern ones.

ZEUS, FATHER OF THE GODS, was originally a god of mountains and weather who lived on a mountain peak and gathered the clouds around himself. When he evolved into the most powerful of the Greek gods, his place of residence naturally had to be changed to the highest Greek mountain, Mount Olympus.

Reconstruction of ancient Olympia. The Temple of Zeus (at center) took over 15 years to build. It was built by the Greek architect Libon of Elis, and dedicated in 456 BC. It was the largest temple on the Greek mainland until the construction of the Parthenon in Athens in 432 BC.

How was the Temple of Zeus at Olympia paid for?

In about 470 BC an appeal for donations went out to all of Greece, to rich and to poor. The goal was to build a temple to the Olympian Zeus, a temple bigger and more splendid than any other in Greece. And the donations came: money, artworks, weapons, jewelry — anything that might help in any way to build a house for Zeus more splendid than anything ever seen before.

The temple was completed and dedicated in 457 BC. It stood on an artificial hill about 3 feet high. The foundation, which has survived virtually intact, measures 206 by 88 feet. On this base stood a total of 34 limestone pillars, each about 30 feet high, that supported the weight of the marble panels that made up the roof.

The core of the temple was the "cella," the sanctuary that contained the statue of Zeus that the sculptor Phidias had created for the temple. This statue is the third of the Seven Wonders of the World and the only one that did not stand under an open sky but rather under the roof of a building. Phidias was an Athenian and is generally considered to be the greatest artist of antiquity. He was commissioned by his friend Pericles to work on the Acropolis, and played a decisive role in both architectural and sculptural matters. In 438 BC he created the statue of Pallas Athena that stood in the Parthenon, one of the most important artworks of its time.

When Phidias was commissioned to create the Olympian Zeus, he first had a studio built. It was located about 260 feet from the temple, and had the same inner dimensions as the cella. Here, with the help of two assistants, he created the statue of Zeus — in a form we know only from ancient

The frieze on the east gable of the Temple of Zeus showed Zeus between Pelops and Oinomaos, two figures from mythology, who stand ready for a chariot race.

Greek coins. Zeus was seated in a high-backed armchair, and in his left hand he held a scepter, a symbol of his power. On the head of the scepter sat his sacred messenger, the eagle. His right hand was extended, face up, and on his open palm stood the winged goddess of victory, Nike. Zeus' head was crowned with a wreath of olive branches, one like the wreath presented to victorious athletes in the

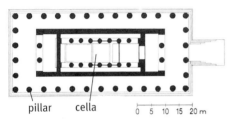

pillar   cella

0 5 10 15 20 m

Floor plan of the Temple of Zeus at Olympia

Olympic Games. The feet of the king of the gods rested on a stool supported by two lions. An inscription on the stool read "Phidias, son of Charmides of Athens, created me."

Working in his studio, Phidias first built a framework of iron, wood, and plaster that roughly corresponded to the figure of Zeus he wanted to create. Then the parts of the body not clothed — the face, arms, hands and feet — were covered with skillfully carved ivory. Throughout Greece the story spread that Zeus had only created elephants so that they could supply the ivory required for the statue. Zeus' hair,

How did Phidias create the statue of Zeus?

his clothing, and his sandals were made of gold. Calculations based on similar works by Phidias suggest that the gold plating for this statue may have weighed around 44 talents — approximately 440 pounds. This would mean that the statue's gold alone would have cost some $3.5 million at today's prices. The eyes of the god were probably precious stones the size of a fist.

Altogether the statue was about 40 feet high. The figure of Nike alone was about the size of a grown man. It was of course impossible to transport this gigantic statue in one piece from the studio to the nearby temple. Phidias probably broke it down into pieces after its completion, and then had these individual parts transported to the cella where they were then put back together to form the mighty image of Zeus.

In the Greece of that time there were many buildings and statues

PHIDIAS lived during what we call the "classical" period of Greek history. It was a golden age for Athens. Athens had created the first democracy; the Athenians built the famous temples on the Acropolis; Aeschylus, Euripides and Sophocles wrote tragedies that are still performed today; the historian Herodotus wrote his record of the known world; the philosopher Socrates engaged Athenians in conversation in the public square; the sculptor Myron first depicted the human body in motion; and the philosopher Democritus developed his theory of atoms as indivisible building blocks of matter.

Phidias' workshop was excavated between 1954 and 1958. It was exactly the same size as the cella of the temple.

that were certainly the equal of Phidias' Zeus in artistic terms. So why was it this statue that was labeled a "Wonder of the World" rather than Phidias' Athena statue, for example, or the Acropolis?

There are two related answers to this question. In the first place, as we have already seen, Olympia was the most important site devoted to the worship of Zeus in all of Greece, and Phidias' statue of Zeus was the largest and best-known image of the highest of the Greek gods. There is another reason, however, that most cultural historians consider even more compelling: in this statue Phidias had created an entirely new image of Zeus. Prior to this time, only the unlimited power and the immortality of the Greek gods had distinguished them from humans. Other than this they were in every sense just like mortals. They were vengeful and vain like humans, treacherous and cruel – even Zeus, the king of the gods, had no qualms about using deceit to win the favor and love of all sorts of women.

The Olympian Zeus made a very different impression. Here sat a wise, old man with a benevolent expression, a god who inspired trust rather than fear, an energetic but loving father. It is understandable, then, that many Greeks felt a particular reverence toward this new Zeus.

Why was the statue of Zeus one of the Seven Wonders?

This was the image of Zeus Greeks had known so far — Zeus hurling lightning bolts. Phidias' statue in the temple at Olympia showed a wise and understanding Zeus.

This bronze coin from around 113 AD shows the head of Phidias' Zeus.

A sesterce from the same period shows the seated Zeus of Olympia.

The athletes regarded the statue as the protector and judge of the games. On the first day of the Games they would go before his altar, offer sacrifices, pray for victory, and vow that they would compete fairly. Then the five-day-long festival began. During the course of the festival young men competed in many different sports, hoping to win an Olympic victory.

The excavations at Olympia began in 1906. The photo shows the foundations of the temple.

The prize the winners received for their victory was a simple olive branch, wound into a wreath. Using a pair of golden scissors, a local boy cut the branch from an olive tree said to have been planted by Hercules, a son of Zeus. This was an expression of the belief that it was not mortals who awarded the prizes, but Zeus himself.

How was an Olympic victor honored?

And so the Olympic Games were held virtually unchanged for more than 1,100 years. Then, in about the middle of the 4th century BC,

Women were only allowed at the games during the victory ceremony, which took place in front of the Temple of Zeus.

monetary prizes were introduced in addition to the olive branch. Instead of amateurs participating in order to honor Zeus, there were now professional athletes — "pros."

Soon after this, Christianity arrived in Greece and Zeus faded into the background. In 393 AD, the Christian emperor Theodosius I condemned the Olympic Games as pagan and forbid any future celebration of the games.

Of the original Olympic complex, only the temple foundation and a few sculptures from the pediment have been found. As for the fate of the statue of Zeus, there are only conjectures. We do know that it was severely damaged in an earthquake in the 2nd century AD. Whether it was then destroyed by looters in 350 AD, as some say, or was taken to Constantinople where a fire destroyed it in 475 AD — as

the other version claims — no one knows. The fate of its creator, Phidias, is also uncertain. It is true that his studio was discovered and excavated in the 19th century, and that archaeologists found several tools that had belonged to him. We will never know, however, whether Phidias died peacefully as an honored artist, or if, as some claim, he died in an Athenian prison after being accused of embezzling gold and ivory.

THE OLIVE TREE is one of the most important plants in the Mediterranean region. Its fruit — the olive — provides oil, and its fine-grained wood is suitable for making furniture. In the ancient Mediterranean world its importance went beyond its practical uses, however. When Noah sent out a dove to see if the floodwaters had receded, the dove brought back an olive leaf. A wreath woven from an olive branch honored Olympic champions. Even today an olive branch is still a symbol of peace.

The Temple of Artemis

THE COAST OF ASIA MINOR and the offshore islands — such as Chios and Samos — were settled by Greeks from the region of Ionia in the 11th century BC. The favorable location of the new Ionian cities on busy trade routes and on the caravan routes from the East brought them great wealth. As a result, their culture flourished. Their authors produced great works of poetry, philosophy, geography, and history. Chios was believed to be the birthplace of the poet Homer. The philosophers Thales and Anaximander were from Miletus, and Heraclitus lived in Ephesus.

Ruins of the ancient city of Ephesus. The road in the picture above once led to a harbor. Time has changed much — today the excavations of Ephesus are many miles inland.

> **How was the famous temple destroyed?**

On a hot summer night in the year 356 BC, a man crept silently through the streets of Ephesus, a city in Asia Minor — present-day Turkey. In his right hand he held a small torch, which he nervously shielded with his wide cloak, hiding it from others who were out that night. Anxiously looking around and avoiding all the main streets, he finally reached a large, white temple at the edge of the city. The temple watchmen were asleep, and so he was able to enter the sanctuary without encountering resistance. Here he did something that horrified the entire civilized world of that time. With the torch he set fire to some wooden cult objects and offerings. The fire spread quickly to the oiled wooden doors and to the curtain covering the statues of the gods. Soon the roof caught fire as well, and within a short time the temple was a smoking ruin. Out of this ruin the marble pillars — some cracked or fallen — rose accusingly into the dark night sky.

In court, where he was sentenced to severe tortures, the man confessed that he had set the temple on fire in order to assure his name a place in history. The Ephesians agreed never to pronounce the name of the mad fame-seeker,

Artemis was worshiped in Ephesus as the goddess of the hunt.

In an attempt to make his name immortal, a fame-seeking Greek named Herostratos set fire to the Temple of Artemis in Ephesus in 356 BC. As the fire burned, the 1,000-year-old building collapsed into a pile of rubble.

so that they could at least deny him the fruit of his crime. Despite their efforts, however — or perhaps, ironically, because of them — we still know his name today: Herostratos. And the temple that he had reduced to ash and rubble was "the greatest, most beautiful, and most noble sanctuary in all the world," as the Greek historian Ampelius wrote. His contemporary Pliny the Younger wrote that it was a "truly admirable monument of Greek splendor." It was the marble temple of Artemis at Ephesus, the fourth of the Seven Wonders of the World.

At that time this sacred place was already more than a thousand years old. Towards the end of the second millennium BC, the Ionians left the Greek mainland and set out in search of new sites for settlements. They traveled to Asia Minor and here some of them founded the city of Ephesus on the coast opposite the island of Samos. The city and harbor quickly developed into a lively center of trade, with beautiful large houses and small huts, clean streets and wide "agorae" (public squares) that were constantly filled with people. Business and trade flourished as they had in their old homeland, Greece. Soon Ephesus was one of the most important cities in the ancient world.

This statue of a mourning Amazon once stood in the Temple of Artemis. The Greek sculptor Cresilas created it as his entry in a contest for the most beautiful statue.

COUNTLESS BUILDINGS and artworks from antiquity have been lost forever. This was only rarely the result of an individual's actions, however, as in the case of the Temple of Artemis. Fire, wars, and earthquakes were the most common destructive forces. Christians and Muslims destroyed "heathen" temples and used them as stone quarries. The few surviving statues are now mostly in museums — and thus saved from complete destruction.

Who was Artemis?

In an isolated place at the mouth of the River Cayster, the settlers found a small enclosure in which a holy tree grew. Here the native inhabitants worshiped an ancient Asiatic nature goddess, a woman with many breasts. The Greeks adopted this cult, but in the female goddess they saw their own Artemis, the virgin goddess of the moon, the mighty huntress, the protector of cities, women, and young animals.

Head of an Amazon from the Artemision

Of course the Greeks didn't think the small sanctuary was enough for their goddess, who was, after all, a daughter of Zeus and the twin sister of Apollo. So they began to build a new temple for Artemis — one that would be bigger, more beautiful, and more magnificent. There was a bit of good fortune mixed with misfortune when Ephesus was conquered by the Lydian king Croesus in 560 BC. Croesus was not only immeasurably wealthy — even today the name "Croesus" is still sometimes used to mean a very rich man — he was also a great admirer of Greek art and the Greek gods. With his financial support the Temple of Artemis was built, the most magnificent sanctuary in the Greek world. It was called the "Artemision."

Since there were often earthquakes in Asia Minor, the temple was deliberately built in a marshy area, since they believed that the soft ground could absorb even violent tremors. First they excavated a large space and rammed charred oak trunks into the floor of the excavation. These trunks supported a massive foundation of rock, which was piled up until it was level with the surrounding ground. The temple was erected on this foundation, and measured 167 feet in width and 344 feet in length. The 127 marble columns were 60 feet high, about the height of a six-story building. The ceilings and roof trusses were made of cedar, and the high double doors leading to the cella were made of polished cypress wood and were richly decorated with gold and a great blaze of color. In the cella stood the statue of Artemis, which was over seven feet tall. It was made of wood from grapevines and covered with silver and gold.

Before the fire, the Artemision looked something like this. It was 167 feet wide and 344 feet long. The roof rested on 127 columns that were nearly 60 feet tall!

With his insane act, the fame-seeking Herostratos had destroyed this unique building and its priceless contents in a matter of minutes — but not entirely. Beneath the shattered columns and the marble statues that had burned to chalk, and among melted vessels and cracked walls, the Ephesians found the statue of Artemis virtually unharmed. It was a miracle, they said, and took it as a sign from the gods that they should rebuild the temple, but even bigger, even more beautiful, and even more magnificent than before.

> **What did the Ephesians find beneath the temple ruins?**

From every corner of Greece and even beyond, offerings poured into Ephesus: gold, jewelry and other offerings, given by both young and old, rich and poor. They began at once to build a new temple.

The Ephesian architect Dinocrates was given the task of building the new temple. Wherever large fragments of the old temple rose out of the rubble, he had them removed; the rest of the debris he had leveled off. This was the new foundation. He then had this foundation enclosed with thick marble blocks, and the base now measured 213 feet by 410 feet. Otherwise, Dinocrates followed the architecture of the original temple. Precisely where the old, cracked pillars had stood, he raised 127 new columns. Again, the lower shafts of 36 of the new pillars bore relief friezes that extended up the pillar to a height greater than that of a fully-grown

Reconstruction of the second Artemision. Croesus donated most of the pillars.

man. These friezes portrayed the deeds of Greek gods and heroes. Over the course of several decades the old temple was built anew, although it was now 7 feet taller than before, since a 7-foot-thick floor had been laid onto the leveled debris that formed the new foundation. There was also another difference: in order to prevent another madman like Herostratos from coming and destroying the temple by fire, this time the roof was not made of wood, but of solid stone.

In 334 BC Alexander the Great arrived in Ephesus in the course of his famous Persian expedition — his triumphal march through Asia Minor. He visited the temple, which was still under construction, and offered his help — advice and

> **Why wasn't Alexander the Great allowed to help build the temple?**

ALEXANDER THE GREAT (356–323 BC) was not Greek but Macedonian. He was, however, educated by the Greek philosopher Aristotle. Alexander is considered the most successful general of ancient times. He crossed the Hellespont — known today as the Dardanelles — with an army of 30,000 men and conquered the Persian Empire. He set up his own extensive empire with Babylon as its capital and Greek as its official language. He also founded several cities that were named after him — for example Alexandria in Egypt. His empire quickly disintegrated, however, when he died of a fever in 323 BC.

Reliefs decorated the bases of the pillars in the second Artemision. Here Hermes, the messenger god, leads the dead into the underworld.

Small ivory statues from the treasure found at Ephesus.

During excavation work at Ephesus in 1903, the British archaeologist Hogarth discovered pieces of jewelry and coins from treasury of the Artemision.

labor, but above all, money. His offer put the Ephesians in a difficult position. On the one hand they didn't want to offend the powerful King of Macedonia, on the other hand, however, he was a "barbarian" – the Greeks at that time considered anyone a barbarian whose native tongue wasn't Greek – and they didn't want to accept help from a barbarian. They found a cunning solution to their problem. A leader and general as powerful as Alexander must be a god, they explained to the foreign king, and it would be inappropriate for a god to build a temple to a goddess. Flattered, Alexander took his army and left.

As with the old Artemision, the construction of the new one took several decades. And again, the temple of Artemis was not just a place of worship. Business great and small was transacted there, wares were bought and sold, and, as was typi-cal in Greece, the temple was the largest and most important bank in town. Anyone who needed money went to the High Priest, who was also a kind of bank director. He loaned money and charged interest, and not at bargain rates. The normal interest rate was 10%, so anyone who wanted to borrow 100 talents had to pay 10 talents a year in interest. Cities and communities got a somewhat better deal – they paid only 6% – and if the state needed money for a new war, the Priest of Artemis charged a mere 1.5%.

In 133 BC, after losing a war against Rome, Ephesus came under Roman rule and was made the capital of the Roman province of Asia. This didn't lessen the city's

This painting from the 17th century shows Artemis – or Diana — hunting.

or the temple's powers of attraction: the Greek goddess Artemis was transformed into the Roman goddess Diana, and Ephesus once again enjoyed a period of great prosperity.

For another three hundred years the Artemision remained a center of religious, intellectual, and commercial life — until 262 AD, when marauding Goths plundered the temple and partially destroyed it. Whatever importance it still had, it lost 118 years later when the Roman emperor Theodosius I made Christianity the state religion and ordered all pagan temples closed. The Artemision had finally become meaningless. Christians, Seljukians, and Arabs took building materials from the temple of Artemis — for churches, mosques, and houses. The Artemision had become little more than a stone quarry.

> **How was the Artemision destroyed?**

Thus this building that had been famous throughout the ancient world gradually disappeared, and with it the old city of Ephesus, which gradually sank into the swamp along the River Cayster. It was later rebuilt above the swamps. When the Ottomans (the Turks) came there in the Middle Ages, the ancient city of Ephesus and its temple had disappeared without leaving a trace. Even the location of the former city and temple had been forgotten.

Around the middle of the 19th century, archaeologists began to search for Ephesus and the Artemision. After years of unsuccessful efforts, the British archaeologist John T. Wood discovered the foundations of the Artemision, buried under 20 feet of mud. In 1903 his colleague David Hogarth found the treasures of Artemis — 3,000 precious pearls, earrings, hairpins, brooches, and small coins made of electron, a mixture of gold and silver. In 1956, archaeologists found Phidias' studio, and in it were three copies of the Artemis statue from the first Artemision. All of these irreplaceable treasures are kept in the museums at Ephesus and Selçuk in present-day Turkey.

MANY GREEK GODS were simply adopted by the Romans. For example, Zeus became Jupiter; his wife Hera became Juno; the sea god Poseidon became Neptune; the war god Ares became Mars; the love goddess Aphrodite became Venus; the messenger god Hermes became Mercury; and Dionysus, the god of wine, became Bacchus.

The Greek goddess of the hunt, Artemis, was called Diana by the Romans.

Where once the Temple of Artemis stood there is now only a swampy lake.

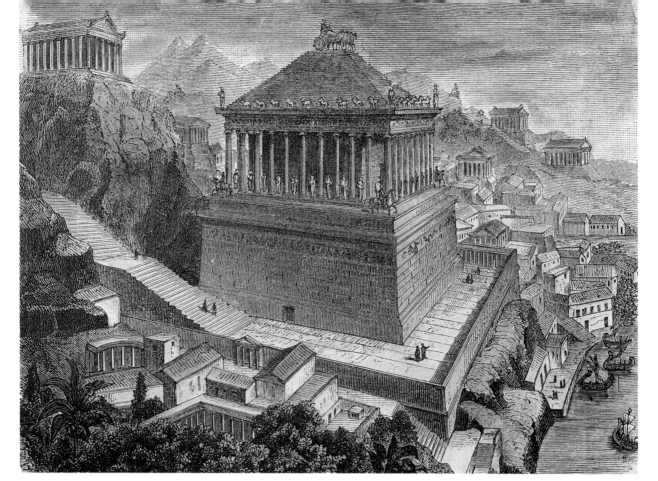

The tomb of Mausolus was completely destroyed. Today the only thing that marks the site are the excavations for the foundation. This reconstruction is from 1890.

The Tomb of Mausolus

About 66 miles south of Ephesus, the home of the fourth Wonder of the World, lies the Turkish town of Bodrum. Two thousand years ago the town was called Halicarnassus, and it was here that the fifth Wonder of the World stood — the tomb of King Mausolus.

Who made Halicarnassus into a great city?

As we mentioned before, towards the end of the second millennium BC, Greeks in search of new places to live left their homeland and traveled to Asia Minor. At this time several new cities were founded, among them Ephesus, Halicarnassus, and — somewhat more inland — Mylasa.

In 546 BC the region fell to the Persian King Cyrus II. The huge Persian Empire now extended from the Mediterranean Sea to the Indus, and from the Black Sea to the Indian Ocean. It was now too big to be ruled centrally. Therefore, the Persian Empire allowed a number of smaller kingdoms to remain somewhat independent — ruled by kings who were subject to the Persian king, but who could otherwise do as they pleased — as long as it didn't go against the interests of the Persian "king of kings." These kings were called "satraps" (governors).

One of the satrapies, as the regions ruled by a satrap were called, was Caria, the coastal area in southwestern Asia Minor. In 400 BC

This statue depicts King Mausolus of Icaria, who died in 352 BC. The 10-foot-high statue was found among the rubble where the Mausoleum once stood. Today it is on display in the British Museum in London.

King Hecatomnus reigned there, a loyal vassal of the Persian ruler, Artaxerxes. Hecatomnus' capital city was Mylasa, located in the mountains above Halicarnassus. He wasn't satisfied with this capital, however, and wanted to move his residence to Halicarnsus. Although Mylasa lay at an important crossroad for many land trade routes, Halicarnassus had an important double harbor that was protected by an island just off-shore. It was also very favorably situated in Asia Minor's coastal trade routes.

Hecatomnus began extensive construction in order to transform the modest harbor town into a residence worthy of a king. He didn't survive to see the move, however. He died in 377 BC, and his eldest son, Mausolus, ascended to the throne.

The young satrap continued his father's work with great energy. He built a strong wall around the entire city, which was built on the mountain slopes around the double harbor like an amphitheater. He had a large agora (public square) built in the center of the city, and, high above the agora, a temple to the war god Ares. Exactly half way between the agora and the temple, Mausolus planned his own tomb, which was meant to preserve his name and his importance for all posterity.

Like almost all Persian kings and satraps, Mausolus was an ardent admirer of Greek art and culture.

How did King Mausolus plan to make his name immortal?

THE PERSIAN EMPIRE came into being under Cyrus the Great who ascended the throne in 558 BC. He first conquered the Medes, then the Babylonians and Asia Minor. A few decades later Darius I consolidated the empire so that it stretched from Asia Minor to the Indus. The key to his success was his army of archers on horses — a military strategy he adopted from the peoples of the Steppes. Regional governors called "satraps" tightly administered the empire with roads ensuring good connections to the central administration. Initial tolerance quickly changed to despotism under Xerxes (about 470 BC) who treated his subjects like slaves.

This relief of an archer comes from the palace of King Darius' at Susa.

Two panels from the 3-foot-high "Amazon frieze" from the Mausoleum — the work of the Greek sculptor Scopas.

THE AMAZONS,

according to Greek legend, were a race of female warriors living somewhere in western Asia. Only in spring did they live for a while with the men of neighboring tribes. Newborn girls were brought up as warriors and trained to use bows and arrows. Boys were sent to live with their fathers or killed. The Amazons were often depicted in artworks and usually shown riding in full battle-dress — in friezes and murals, on vases, and in more modern times in paintings.

So instead of having his tomb designed by native architects, he invited all Greek artists to take part in a competition to design the most beautiful tomb.

There was hardly a single Greek architect of any importance who didn't take part in the competition. Since 404, when the Spartan general Lysander conquered Athens and made himself ruler of all Greece, there had been little work for Hellenic artists. Cities and communities were too poor to give work to architects, sculptors, goldsmiths, or other artisans. Greek architects were therefore grateful for this opportunity, even if it did come from an "outsider" — a "barbarian."

What did Mausolus' tomb look like?

The architects Satyrus and Pythius won the competition. Their design looked like this: on top of a five-tiered base that measured 108 feet by 128 feet, stood an enormous block approximately 88 feet wide and 108 feet long. The base and block together rose to a height of 72 feet. On top of this came the actual funerary temple. Thirty-nine pillars, each 36 feet high, surrounded its cella or interior. The cella and the aisle of pillars surrounding it — the peristyle — supported a 24-tiered pyramid that formed the roof of the monument. The pyramid was crowned by a marble quadriga — a chariot drawn by four horses. The entire tomb

Fragment of one of the horses from the quadriga on the Mausoleum.

was 160 feet tall — taller than a present-day 16-story building. The tomb was very unusual for its time, you could even say it was revolutionary: the dominant style in Greek architecture emphasized horizontal forms, that is, forms that were longer and wider than they were tall. Mausolus' tomb, in contrast, towered upwards. It was also unusual since the Greeks didn't build tombs for their dead. Even their most revered dead were buried in the ground. Mausolus, however, had his final resting place designed so that it towered up into the heavens, just as the Egyptians had done thousands of years before with their pyramids, and as some Persians had done with their raised tombs. Mausolus' tomb was thus a mixture of Greek, Egyptian, and Persian architectural styles. This combination was later adopted by many cultures. Since that time, important figures have often been buried in similar tombs. We call these tombs "mausoleums," after the builder of the first such tomb.

The world's first mausoleum did not become the fifth Wonder of the World solely because of its unusual architecture, however. Outstanding sculptors created the reliefs and friezes that decorated the tomb — unique works of art, which amazed the world. They portrayed chariot races, battling Amazons, gods, and other mythological figures — the marble figures were a mirror of the ancient world.

Mausolus never saw these masterpieces, however. He died in 353, before they were finished. Mausolus' wife, Artemisia, who deeply loved her husband, continued the work. She wasn't just Mausolus' wife, she was also his sister. She was very young when she married her oldest brother, whom she adored. In doing so, Artemisia was following the example of the Egyptian pharaohs, who often married their sisters, since along the Nile the line of succession went through the eldest daughter and not through the sons.

In completing the tomb, Artemisia also left a memorial to herself. There was not just one driver guiding the four horses of the quadriga, there were two holding the reins, a man and a woman — Mausolus and Artemisia. According to authors from that time, however, the deceased king probably wouldn't have approved of the queen leaving herself a memorial in this way.

Again and again artists have given their imagination free rein when attempting to reconstruct King Mausolus' tomb. This engraving was made in the 18th century.

In the 15th century, the cru-saders of the Order of St. John of Jerusalem took large parts of the Mausoleum ruins and used them in building the fortification of St. Peter.

ARTEMISIA, the wife and sister of Mausolus, was a bold and intelligent woman. After Mausolus' death Halicarnas-sus was attacked by ships from Rhodes – the people of Rhodes believed they could easily conquer Artemisia. Artemisia, however, defeated them with cunning. When the soldiers from Rhodes went on land, she had their ships towed out to open sea. They panicked, since their retreat had been cut off, and were de-feated.

Who completed the tomb after Mausolus' death?

Like her husband, however, Artemisia did not live to see the completion of the tomb. She died only two years after her husband and brother. At this point it was un-certain whether the building would ever be completed. Sculp-tors, architects, and other crafts-men who had been working on the building took the initiative. They felt that such a unique building could not be left unfinished. It was built "for all eternity," and therefore had to be completed, even without the ones who com-missioned it. "For all eternity" — at first it seemed this was true. Alexander the Great laid siege to Halicarnassus in 334 BC and de-stroyed the city, but Mausolus' tomb remained unharmed. It also survived the fortunes of subse-quent wars undamaged. The "eternity" lasted for 1,500 years. In the 12th century AD large parts of the structure collapsed during an earthquake. Three hundred years later, Crusaders used the ru-ins as a quarry for stone to build fortifications against the ap-proaching Turks. When they were through, the Mausoleum had been leveled to the ground — only foun-dations remained.

In 1523 the army of the Turkish sultan Suleiman the Magnificent occupied Halicarnassus. Where the Mausoleum had once stood, they built villas for the conquerors. In 1857 British archaeologists bought 12 of these villas and excavated what was left of the Mausoleum. These artifacts — tokens of "that precious stroke of fortune," as a Roman poet once described the Mausoleum — are now among the most valuable objects in the British Museum in London.

The Colossus of Rhodes

Why did King Demetrius lay siege to the city of Rhodes?

King Demetrius, seated in his battle tent, was furious. This warrior, generally known as "Poliorcetes" — the besieger of cities — had been trying for several weeks to take the city of Rhodes on the island of the same name. Even his bravest soldiers could not get past the wall that protected the city and its harbor.

It was the year 305 BC, and Demetrius, King of Phrygia and Lycia in Asia Minor, had asked the people of Rhodes to support him in his battles against the Egyptian ruler, Ptolemy Soter. They refused, however, since they didn't want to wage war against their most important trading partner. Therefore, Demetrius now tried to bring Rhodes under his control before he attacked Alexandria.

It was true that he had been able to gain a foothold on the island and bring troops, weapons and provisions on land, but now even the most violent attacks were rebuffed at the wall surrounding the city and harbor. The citizens of Rhodes were willing to fight to the death to defend their city.

What was the largest war machine of all times?

In order to conquer Rhodes, Demetrius had an enormous siege tower built, the biggest instrument of war ever seen up to that time. "Helepolis" (=city destroyer) was about 100 feet high, a wheeled oak tower nine stories tall, with ramming rods and catapults that could hurl 200-pound stones hundreds of yards. It was said that it took 3,400 men to move this giant. In the upper stories there was also an army of archers protected by barricades and ready to shower the enemy with arrows. These upper floors also had drawbridges that could be let down onto the city wall, thus enabling the army to occupy the wall. In order to protect

Since no authentic images of the Colossus of Rhodes have survived, the giant statue has been portrayed in many different ways. Today historians no longer believe that the giant statue straddled the entrance to the harbor, as depicted in this engraving from 1790. The statue probably stood somewhere in the city itself.

Helepolis broke through the city walls of Rhodes.

SIEGES were the most common method of making war from ancient times up to the early nineteenth century. Attacking troops would first encircle a town or fort. In most cases, if this was kept up for a few weeks or months and combined with some shooting, it was all that was necessary. Hunger, thirst, and disease forced the defenders to surrender. If this did not work, then attackers would try to break through the protective walls using heavy siege equipment such as battering rams, movable wooden towers, or artillery.

the wooden tower from the flaming arrows of the enemy, they had stretched animal hides over a frame of woven willow branches. They sprayed water over the hides constantly.

The monster succeeded on its first attempt. The soldiers pushed it up against the wall and it broke a wide hole through it. Instead of pushing on further, however, the besieging army decided to delay the attack on the inner city until the following morning.

Earlier in the day, as the people of Rhodes saw the monster rolling closer and closer to the city ramparts, they fell onto their knees and prayed to Helios, the god and protector of their city. They vowed they would build a statue of him even taller than Helepolis, if he would save them in their time of need.

And Helios did help. He gave them the idea of digging a deep trench directly behind the city wall, opposite the siege tower, and camouflaging it with branches and earth.

The trench worked as they had hoped it would. The next morning when Helepolis began to move, it moved only a yard or two before its front wheels sank into the trench and the tower could no longer move. The war machine now blocked the opening it had made in the city wall the previous day.

After this failure, Demetrius abandoned his attempt to take Rhodes. He signed a peace treaty with the city and withdrew. The people of Rhodes then began to build the statue of Helios in fulfillment of their vow. This statue became the sixth Wonder of the World.

Why was Helios the patron god of Rhodes?

Why, when they needed help, did the people of Rhodes pray to Helios out of all the many Greek gods? We find an answer in Greek mythology. On the morning when the king of gods, Zeus, divided up the earth among the gods, the sun god Helios wasn't present. He was still on his daily journey across the expanse of heaven, driving his golden quadriga with its white sun-horses. As compensation for being left out, Helios demanded that Zeus give him an island that he had seen under the water, slowly rising — the island of Rhodes. Zeus agreed, and from that time forth, on the sunny island of Rhodes, Helios held a special place among all the Greek gods. And so

Head of a statue of Helios

the people of the island rushed to fulfill their promise to him.

In doing so, they also proved what shrewd merchants they were. They commissioned the highly respected sculptor Chares of Lindos to make a 60-foot-high statue. They reached an agreement with the artist for a fixed price covering both work and materials. Later, however, they asked that the statue be made twice as large, and Chares, who was apparently not very good at mathematics, simply doubled the price they had agreed upon. Only later did he realize that the people of Rhodes had played him for a fool. In reality, the cost for work and materials was eight times higher. Chares went bankrupt fulfilling his contract, and after spending twelve years completing

THE SUN GOD HELIOS traveled across the heavens each day, from east to west, on a golden chariot pulled by four fire-breathing, winged horses. At least this is how the ancient Greeks imagined the sun moved. Then at night he returned across the ocean to his palace in the East, sailing in a golden cup. Selene, the moon Goddess, was sometimes said to be his wife.

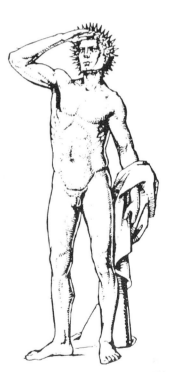

This attempt at a reconstruction of the 104-foot-high sun god is based on the descriptions of writers who lived during the time the statue was created.

This Greek vase depicts Helios, the sun god, as he drives across the heavens in his chariot with its four fiery steeds.

tach the huge bronze segments to the rough form. Historians don't know whether the bronze was cast or hammered into shape. All in all the construction is said to have used more than 12 tons of bronze, which would mean that the walls of the statue had an average thickness of six hundredths of an inch (0.06 inches). In order to stabilize the statue, the workers filled it up to the head with rocks. Only a narrow shaft in the interior of the Colossus was left unfilled. A wooden ladder ran through the shaft up to the head, so that repairs could be made.

A statue of this size is unusual even in our times. As a comparison: Helios would tower over the Statue of Liberty by 35 feet. The fingers of the statue were more than six feet long, and so thick that you couldn't reach both arms around them.

How big was the statue of Helios?

There are no surviving images of the Helios statue, not even on coins — we know only from written reports what it may have looked like. The figure stood on a pedestal and was probably naked. Helios either had his right hand resting against his forehead, as if he were thinking, or he was holding a torch. His garment hung over his left forearm — or, according to another description, he held an arrow in his left hand, for the bow hanging over his shoulder. The only thing we know for sure is that his face and the crown on his head — with its seven sunrays — were covered with gold.

Inside the 104-foot-high Helios there was an inner frame made of iron. It was first covered in clay and then encased in thin bronze plates.

the statue of Helios, he committed suicide.

The work began in 302 BC. First of all, Chares built an iron framework to support the statue from within. He covered it with clay. This rough form had almost the same measurements as the final version. A wall of earth was then built up around the form in the shape of a rising spiral. From this platform the workers could at-

We don't really know where the statue stood. Recent research suggests it is very unlikely that the statue straddled the harbor entrance, as many used to think. Today historians think the statue probably stood in the city, facing east — that is, toward the starting point of Helios' daily journey across the heavens.

In any case, it only remained standing for 66 years. During an earthquake in 224 BC, Helios broke at the knees and his body came crashing down. The falling statue probably destroyed several of the houses that surrounded it.

Since an oracle had stated that Rhodes would suffer great misfortune if the statue were rebuilt, it was left lying where it had fallen for almost 900 years. When Arabs conquered the island of Rhodes in

Entrance to the harbor at Mandraki on the Greek island of Rhodos. In the background you can see the fortress of St. Nicholas. Historians used to think the Colossus stood here.

653 AD, however, they showed little respect for the fallen Greek god. They tore the bronze covering from the statue and transported it — 900 camel loads — to Edessa, an ancient city in northern Mesopotamia. There it was melted down. And so, from the sixth, and most short-lived of the World Wonders, only the word "colossus" remains.

THE ISLAND OF RHODES lies off the southwest coast of Turkey. It was an important commercial center in ancient times. It became the headquarters of the Knights of Saint John of Jerusalem during the Middle Ages. Today its beaches have made it a popular tourist destination.

THE WORD "COLOSSUS" originally meant simply "statue" in Greek. The meaning we know today, that of "something of great size or scope" or simply a "gigantic statue," was inspired by the huge statue of Helios on Rhodes.

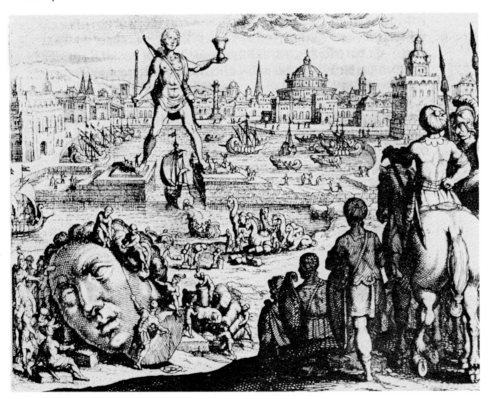

In his collection of engravings showing scenes from history, Matthäus Merian included this depiction of the city of Rhodes. It shows the version of the Colossus current in the 17th century. The collection of engravings was published in 1668.

The Pharos of Alexandria

THE CITY OF ALEXANDRIA was famous throughout the ancient world for its library. There, on more than 700,000 papyrus rolls, the complete knowledge of ancient times was stored. Important scholars worked here — until this irreplaceable treasury of knowledge was destroyed by fire in 391 AD.

Who founded Alexandria?

The seventh Wonder of the World, the Lighthouse at Alexandria, is actually the eighth. Before it was built, the walls of the city of Babylon were listed as the second Wonder. The 430-foot-high lighthouse at the mouth of the Nile River impressed the ancient world so much that people immediately

April, 331 BC — this young world conqueror ordered a ceremonial procession in which he paced off a rectangle measuring 30 stadiums by 7 stadiums. A "stadium" was a Greek measure of distance — distances in races were measured in "stadiums," which is where we get the modern sense of "stadium." In modern terms the rectangle was 5,872 yards by 1,370 yards. Behind Alexander a priest scattered barley flour in the king's footsteps. The oracle had stated that barley flour would incline the gods to be merciful and make it possible for the king's plan to succeed. For here, on the westernmost point of the Nile Delta, the city of Alexandria would rise, the first city founded by the great ruler. He would later found many others in the Near East. By building Alexandria, the Macedonian king hoped to open Egypt to Greek culture and commerce. The city was to become an important trading center and harbor.

After Alexander the Great conquered Egypt, he not only chose the site where the city bearing his name should be built, he also designed its layout. He chose a reef next to the island of Pharos as the site for the lighthouse that was to become the Seventh Wonder of the World.

struck the Babylonian walls from the list and replaced them with this newest wonder. And it remains to this day the tallest lighthouse ever built.

In 332 BC Alexander the Great conquered Egypt and was crowned Pharaoh in the ancient capital city Memphis. He was 24 years old. One year later — on the 16th of

Who designed the layout of the city?

Alexander himself drew up the plans for the city. He chose the sites for the agora and for the trading center. He even determined the number and the locations of the temples to be built, and decided to which Greek

The lighthouse at Alexandria – here in a reconstruction from the 18th century – must have cast a bright light over the harbor when the fire was lit at night.

PHAROS

Since there were no "lighthouses" before the construction of the Alexandrian tower, and therefore no word for such a thing, the tower was originally called simply "Pharos," after the place where it stood. The Roman languages subsequently took up this name. "Lighthouse" in Latin is "pharus," in Italian and Spanish it is "faro," in French "phare," and in Portuguese "farol."
In addition to the name, the gigan-

tic World Wonder also gave the world an architectural custom: towers built in the sequence "four-sided, eight-sided, round" can still be found today.

god each should be dedicated. Finally, he also ordered the construction of a lighthouse on a reef next to the island of Pharos, just opposite Alexandria – a lighthouse that was to be bigger and taller than any previous lighthouse.

Alexandria became all that the king had hoped. Within a short time it was a flourishing city of 600,000 inhabitants, mainly Greek immigrants, Egyptians, and Jews. It became the most important metropolis on the Mediterranean. Alexander, however, never saw the lighthouse. He died in 323, before construction had even begun. It did not begin until 23 years later.

It was a massive structure. On a base that measured 100 feet by 100 feet, builders constructed a 233-foot-high rectangular block that tapered slightly toward the top. On the top surface they erected the second section of the tower, an octagonal structure 111 feet high, and on top of this a round structure, which housed the lighting apparatus. Pillars resting on this round structure supported a cone-shaped roof. Crowning the structure was a stat-

ue of Zeus, who, from a height of 425 feet, looked out over the sea.

The lower part of the tower was divided into 14 vaulted chambers one above another. A gently rising ramp ran along the inside walls. It was so wide that two pack animals could walk side-by-side on it. In the center of the tower there was a shaft that extended from the cellar to the lighting apparatus. A rope drawn lift made it possible to transport materials up into the highest floors. The exterior of the tower was clad in white marble. The structure is said to have cost around 800 talents — about 45,600 pounds of silver. At today's prices that would be about 4.7 million dollars.

The archaeologist Hermann Thiersch drew this reconstruction of the 430-foot-high lighthouse at Alexandria.

Like all naval signals of the time, the lighthouse at Alexandria was probably first planned as a day tower. In those days, ships looked for a safe harbor every evening to avoid being on the sea at night. The harbor at Alexandria grew more rapidly than expected, however. In the inner harbor, grains and vegetables from the fertile Nile Valley were unloaded. In the larger port further out to sea, ships landed with cargoes of wine from Greece, spices from the Orient, metal from Spain, and other goods from all over the world. They also brought passengers with them. There were students who wanted to study astronomy or philosophy at the excellent university that had recently been founded. There were patients who hoped for a cure from the famous Alexandrian doctors. There were also diplomats and merchants, and of course travelers who simply wanted to come and admire the new city on the Nile. Alexandria exported primarily glass, papyrus, and linen.

When sea traffic became too busy, ships had to cast off and sail even at night. For their sake the city installed a powerful lighting apparatus in the tower. It burned oil and tree resin. Wood was too expensive. It had to be imported and was only used for the construction of houses and ships. This was in fact the very first navigational light in the history of maritime travel. The tower at Alexandria was, in the true sense of the word, the very first "lighthouse."

The light was concentrated and reflected by a concave mirror. Reports claim that it was so strong that it could be seen "to the ends of the world." Besides the tower's daring construction, this powerful light was certainly one of the reasons that the lighthouse was added to the list of the Seven Wonders immediately after its completion in 279 BC.

For almost a thousand years the lighthouse at Alexandria survived all the fortunes of wars unharmed. Finally, however, it too succumbed to a fate suffered by other Won-

This is how one artist — about 200 years ago — pictured the Pharos of Alexandria.

This Roman coin bears the image of the Pharos. It dates from the reign of Emperor Domitian (81–96 AD).

In 1480 the Mamluk sultan Qa' it Bay built a fort on the old foundations of the lighthouse. The fort is still standing today and bears the sultan's name.

ders of the World. In 796 AD it collapsed during an earthquake. Attempts by Arabs to rebuild it failed, and in 1480 the Mamluk sultan Qa'it Bay built a fortress on the old foundations. It still stands today and bears the sultan's name.

Index